TOUCHDOWN

Author

Stephen Byers

Photography

Heinz Kluetmeier
Vernon Biever

WATERLOO LOCAL SCHOOL
PRIMARY LIBRARY

©Advanced Learning Concepts, Inc., 1975

Copyright © 1975 by Advanced Learning Concepts, Inc.

International copyrights reserved in all countries.

No part of this book may be reproduced in any form whatsoever without the written permission of the publisher.

Library of Congress Number: 75-1127

ISBN 0-8172-0219-6

Published by **Advanced Learning Concepts, Inc.**
Milwaukee, Wisconsin

A Product of **Advanced Learning Concepts, Inc. and Follett Publishing Company**
A Division of Follett Corporation
Chicago, Illinois

Contents

1	A Hard Man	6
2	The Icebox Game	14
3	Football Under Attack	24
4	The Danger	32
5	Why Do They Play?	42
6	Winners...And Losers	52
	Pre-Reading Aids	65
	Discussion Questions	72
	Related Activities	73

1
A Hard Man

The Green Bay Packers had a big game coming up in a few days. It was pouring rain, and it looked as if their practice might be rained out. Packer Coach Vince Lombardi glared at the sky and yelled: "Stop raining! Stop raining!" There was a flash of lightning and a clap of thunder. It stopped raining.

At least that's how the players tell it. The story is believed throughout football because the players and coaches can't imagine anyone — even Mother Nature — disobeying Vince Lombardi.

That's because Lombardi was a hard, hard man. Some people thought he ate nails for breakfast, rocks for lunch, and football helmets for dinner. Two-hundred-fifty-pound football players were terrified of him. The Lombardi stare was said to be enough to curdle blood at one hundred paces.

It wasn't because Lombardi was huge. He was short, stocky, and always seemed rumpled. It was because he was tough. You failed to listen to him at your own risk. Once he chased tackle Steve Wright across a field after pounding him with his fists. It didn't matter that Wright outweighed Lombardi by eighty pounds.

When Lombardi yelled at you, it seemed like the whole town could hear. He believed in

7

pushing players to their limits — and then beyond. At one practice, he picked out lineman Jerry Kramer. "You run like an old cow, Kramer," he yelled. "You're the worst guard I've ever seen. Keep running and lose some of that baby fat." But after the practice, Lombardi told Kramer: "Son, one of these days you're going to be the greatest guard in the league."

Green Bay had hired the fearsome Lombardi almost in desperation. The season before had been the Packers' worst in history. They won one game, tied one, and lost ten.

Lombardi had been an assistant coach for the New York Giants and before that with Fordham and Army. He hadn't been a head coach since he had coached a high school team.

But Green Bay gave him a chance. The Packer players soon learned that Lombardi didn't mean to blow it. On only the second day of practice, one Packer was stunned when Lombardi fined him fifty dollars for being five minutes late at bed check.

He didn't stop there. He got rid of twelve veteran Packers before his first game. He introduced the players to his form of conditioning: tough drills over and over in the hot summer sun. He didn't allow drinking water at practice. He yelled at players who reported minor injuries. "Lombardi has the highest tolerance of pain of us all," one player said. "Our injuries don't hurt him a bit."

He never stopped pushing the players. Kramer lost seven pounds in one of the early practices. "Lombardi plays no favorites," tackle Henry Jordan said. "He treats us all like dogs."

But the Packers, under Lombardi's whip, changed from the licked group he had taken over. "He tolerates perfection, providing it is real good," one player said. And the Packers

began to look for that perfection within themselves.

It didn't take long for them to begin to find it. In Lombardi's first game as head coach, the Packers faced their archrival, the Chicago Bears.

The Bears were expected to win the division that year. But they couldn't dent Green Bay's defense. In fact, the mighty Bears got inside the twenty yard line only once, and then had to settle for a seventeen-yard field goal.

The Packers, meanwhile, were cashing in on the sweat of the practice field. They were in good condition, so their strength held up. They controlled the game and beat the Bears, 9-6.

As the players carried Lombardi off the field that day in 1959, they had something to think about. In one afternoon they had equalled their one victory of the year before.

After beating the Bears, the Packers upset the Detroit Lions and the San Francisco 49ers before losing a game. The new spirit was strong. The Pack soared to a 7-5 record that season, their best since 1944. Lombardi was named coach of the year in his first year. Even bigger things lay ahead.

The Packers were winning because they had learned Lombardi's lessons well. Lombardi polished the ball-control game to its highest point. What that means is basic, muscle football. Not much passing, a lot of running. Hammering, pounding, plodding along until you have a touchdown.

The big play in Lombardi's bag was the power sweep. On that play, both guards and one back would clear a path around end. The ball carrier would follow them. Lombardi made the Packers practice the power sweep time and time and time again. And when they had it down perfectly, he made them practice it some more. With the power sweep, the Packers steamrolled people.

"Our opponents know what's coming," Lombardi said, "but they can't stop us."

Lombardi also pushed defense. Tackling practice in Green Bay was a crunching, punishing experience both for ball carriers and tacklers. But in games it was the other teams who suffered the punishment at the hands of the stingy Green Bay defense.

Lombardi's style was simple: When the Packers had the ball, the other team couldn't score. His teams were among the first to use ball-control tactics such as those that dominate football today. In almost every game, the Packers ran far more plays than their opponents — and usually scored more points.

Lombardi's lumbering offense and stonewall defense resulted in football that was dull to watch. The scores of games the Packers played dropped sharply. Lombardi played only for his team to win — and that wasn't by scores like 42-38 that other teams rolled up.

It was dull, but it was winning. And that is what football was all about. Fans flocked to watch Lombardi's team play. And other coaches watched jealously — and copied his style.

What Lombardi is most remembered for is an extremely heavy emphasis on winning.

Once he was asked what he wanted to do in football. "That's easy," he replied, "to win, to win, to win." Winning was the only thing, Lombardi said. As he told his players, "I'm here because we win. You're here because we win. When we lose, we're gone."

2
The Icebox Game

The phone rang in the football player's motel room. He woke up on the third ring and picked up the receiver. The cheerful voice of the wake-up girl said:

"Good morning. It is eight a.m. and the temperature is sixteen degrees below zero."

Welcome to Green Bay, Wisconsin. The wake-up girl was a Packer fan. The player was one of the Dallas Cowboys. She wasn't going to let him forget that icy Green Bay was Packer country, not the sunny South where the Cowboys were used to playing in warm weather.

It's not much fun to play football when it's that cold. Hands can't get a good grip on the ball. Flying feet slide on frozen turf. The kind of football that wins in cold weather is tough, simple, power football.

And that was Lombardi's Packers.

Football games, even championship games, slip quickly from memory. They become a blur of guys trotting in and out of huddles. Of big linemen crashing into each other. Of fast backs running for touchdowns.

But this game — the NFL championship game in frozen Green Bay on December 31, 1967 — is remembered. Maybe it's remembered because of the cold. But maybe it's

WATERLOO LOCAL SCHOOL
PRIMARY LIBRARY

remembered because it was Lombardi's Packers against the Dallas Cowboys.

The Dallas team was nearly everything that Lombardi preached against. It relied on fancy passing and the big play for a quick touchdown. Defensive backs gambled. They tried to intercept passes instead of just knocking passes down.

The Cowboys' speed was awesome. "Bullet" Bob Hayes and Pete Gent were two of the best receivers around. Dallas quarterback Don Meredith was outstanding.

The Dallas Doomsday Defense was anchored by Bob Lilly and Jethro Pugh. They were a pair of mountains in a line that was almost impossible to move against.

The Packers were the defending champions. But that was only because the clock had run out on a last-ditch Dallas drive that ended a foot from the goal line the year before.

Lombardi's team was successful — but dull. Plod, plod, plod. Grind, grind, grind. But every Dallas play was a potential scoring play. The Cowboys had style and class. They played with grace and beauty.

So the game would be a clash between simple, conservative football and the flashy game. The game influenced other coaches and teams for years.

By game time it had warmed up — to thirteen below. With the fifteen-mile-an-hour wind, it was like forty-nine degrees below zero on bare skin. The ground felt like a concrete playground.

Millions of people watched the game on television in warm living rooms. Thousands, bundled in heavy layers of coats and sweaters, shivered in the stands. The players had only their uniforms to keep them warm. Some wore gloves, others didn't.

And among those who didn't were most of the Packers. Lombardi didn't like gloves.

The first time the Packers got the ball, they drove eighty-two yards for a touchdown. The steamroller was rolling.

Early in the second quarter, bam! The Packers scored again. From the Dallas forty-three yard line, Bart Starr flipped a short pass to end Boyd Dowler. The lanky Dowler stretched hard to grab the pass. He gathered it in, then loped downfield for a touchdown. Green Bay 14 — Dallas 0.

And an icy chill struck the thousands of Dallas fans watching on television. The Packers were ahead 14-0! Could anyone come back against the awesome Pack — especially playing in the icebox that was Lambeau Field?

Suddenly Dallas came alive. With four minutes left in the first half, a Dallas pass rush worked to perfection. Starr was hit hard, and the ball was jarred loose on the Green Bay seven yard line. George Andrie, a huge defensive lineman, scooped up the ball and carried it over for the first Dallas score. Green Bay 14 — Dallas 7. Then, with just a minute and fifty seconds left in the first half, Dallas kicked a field goal. Green Bay 14 — Dallas 10.

The third quarter was a defensive struggle. Dallas threatened twice, but the Packer defense stopped both drives.

In the fourth quarter, lightning struck.

Dallas had the ball at the fifty yard line. The call was a typical Dallas play — a halfback option pass. Dan Reeves took a handoff and raced outside. Then he threw a long pass upfield. It was complete. Touchdown! Dallas led, 17-14.

A Packer field goal try was short. Then Dallas ate up almost five minutes on running plays before finally punting.

Last chance for the Packers. With time running out, they battered their way to the Dallas one foot line.

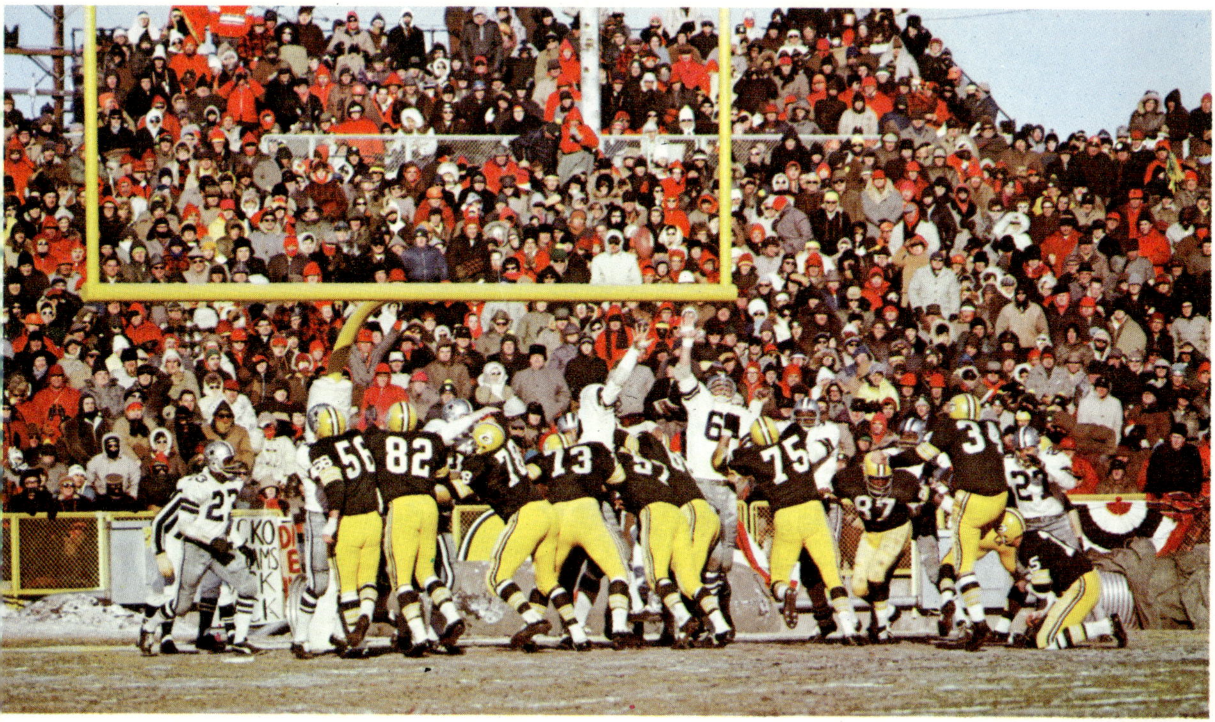
56
82
73
75
87

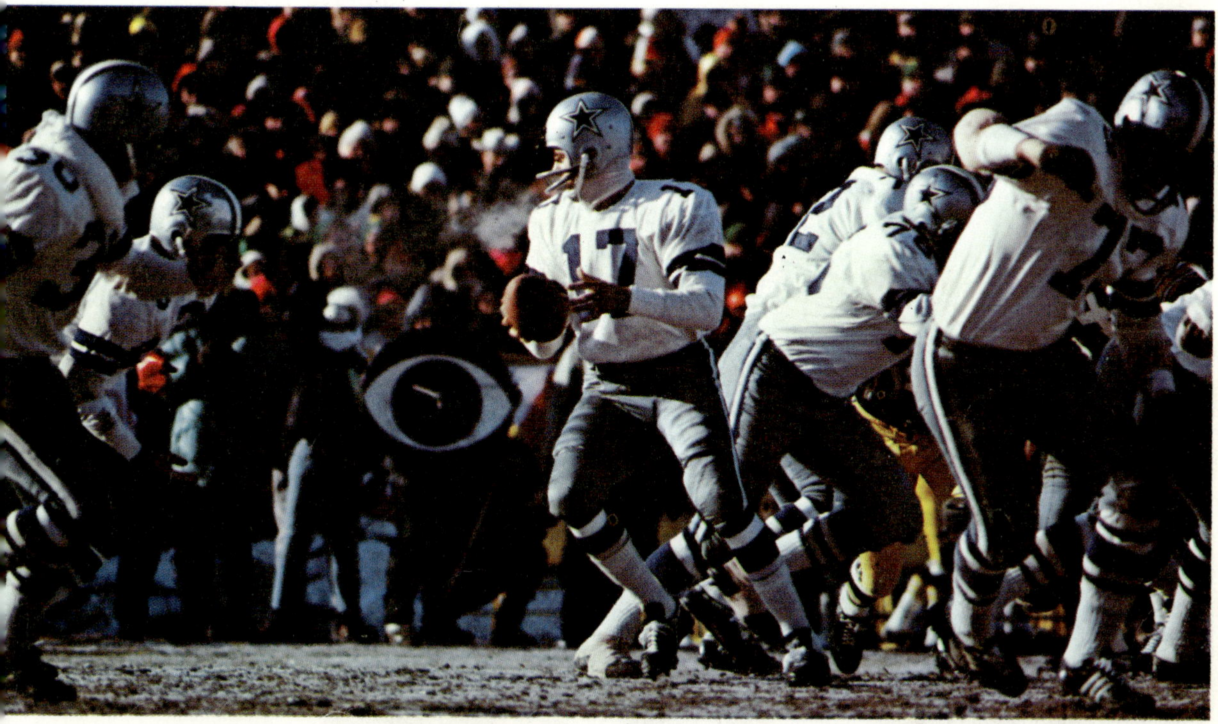

And now Lombardi's teachings would be put to the test. Twice the Packers tried to ram the ball in. And twice they failed. Then, with sixteen seconds left, it was score or else. A whole season was rolled up in one play.

The Packers could be expected to choose a simple play. But the simple play they chose was a surprise. It was a quarterback sneak. They hadn't used that play all year. Bart Starr was to carry the ball through a hole in the line. Guard Jerry Kramer and center Ken Bowman were to make the hole.

Bowman snapped the ball to Starr and then joined Kramer in hitting Pugh. Crunch! The hole in the line was narrow, maybe too narrow to get through. Starr lunged. He landed under a big pile of Cowboys and Packers.

The referee signaled a touchdown.

More than fifty thousand fans shouted for joy and headed for a warmer place — any warmer place. On the sideline, Lombardi smiled.

What goes through a player's mind when a championship hangs on one play? How does he remember it? If he's a winner, he remembers a lot about it. If he lost, he probably remembers it, too. But he'd rather not.

Jethro Pugh lost. For him it was quite simple. "They put a good block on me and drove me back. I was surprised that Starr kept the ball. I expected Donny Anderson to try the middle one more time."

Starr said: "I decided on a quarterback sneak because our backs just weren't getting good footing." Starr, in fact, doesn't talk much about the play. He'd rather talk about the plays that got the Packers to the one foot line. Kramer and Bowman both thought only about Pugh. About moving him out. Both were more concerned about footing on the frozen field than anything else.

In fact, that's what most of the players thought about during the game. Dallas quar-

terback Don Meredith summed it up for the Cowboys: "Minus thirteen. It just wasn't a test of football. You couldn't do the things you want to in weather like this."

But Lombardi didn't think the cold was a factor. "It's a great day," he told the players before the game. And afterward, he claimed that the cold was the same for both teams. The Cowboys scoffed at that. One of them said: "That's like watching a shark and a man fight in the water and saying it's just as wet for the man."

Still, the game was a triumph of the Lombardi style of push and pull, smash and bash.

The Packers went on to their second straight Super Bowl victory and their third straight world championship. In his nine years with the Packers, Lombardi pushed his team to six divisional titles, five league championships, and two Super Bowl victories.

Surely that record showed that winning football meant steady, grinding football. Surely, it meant that stiff rules had to be set and enforced by a heavy-handed coach.

And surely that record showed that Lombardi's way of looking at football was the only way to look at it.

Or did it?

3
Football Under Attack

"To win, to win, to win."

That was the philosophy of Vince Lombardi. Lombardi didn't invent winning-at-all-costs. But he was a kind of high priest of the idea. That's because he carried it to its highest point. He won. He told players they had to play with injuries. But he won. He made a lot of players dislike him. But he won.

Coaches at all levels, from pro to grade school, tried to be more like Lombardi. They pushed simple, tough, winning football. Some tried to push their players like Lombardi pushed his — by humiliation, by making fun of those who didn't measure up.

Just about the time Lombardi was winning championships at Green Bay, people in America were starting to question a lot of things. They questioned war. They questioned products companies sold to the public. And they questioned sports. Particularly football.

Among the people who questioned football the hardest were some of the players. The player who had the most to say against football was the bearded Dave Meggysey. Meggysey was no failure. He was a good linebacker for the St. Louis Cardinals. When he spoke out, people listened.

Meggysey quit football because he didn't like what it had become. And he sounded off a lot about things he felt were wrong in football.

He said there was more to football than just winning. He said most of the people in football were missing the point.

"Too many rules," he said. There were rules on what pro players should wear off the field, rules on how they should act in public, rules on when they had to go to bed. A lot of players hated the bedtime rule. They believed that grown men shouldn't be forced to go to bed by eleven o'clock. George Blanda had to obey the bedtime rule when he was forty-seven years old.

The rules were part of the idea that without dedication and discipline you couldn't win. Dedication and discipline. They sound good. A person needs both to make good in almost any profession. But to some players they became bad words. "Coaches talk of the need for discipline," Meggysey said, "but what they really mean is obedience."

Another thing a lot of people, including some players, didn't like was that coaches expected players to be brutal. John McMurtry, a player in the Canadian Football League, said that what coaches wanted most was a player who could "hit to kill," even if only half his limbs are working.

And some pros worried about kids who were being influenced by the violent image of football.

A lot of coaches drilled their players as if they were commandos being trained for jungle warfare. Some high school coaches would yell at linemen: "Hurt that man across from you!" or "Rip his head off!"

At one high school practice, the coach was watching in disgust. A big sophomore tackle was having a tough time blocking a kid about twenty pounds lighter than he was.

The coach went over to the tackle and roared at him: "Football is not a game for nice people! You've gotta be mean! You've gotta hate him! Imagine that he just killed your sister! You want to destroy him!"

That, Meggysey felt, was what was wrong with football. It had become animalistic. Dehumanizing.

"It's not fair for the thirteen-year-old sandlotter to be expected to play like a pro," one pro player said. And it wasn't just the violence he was talking about. It was also the pressure put on the youngsters to win. A college coach once said that his team was nothing if it wasn't Number One in the national polls. There is, of course, nothing wrong with trying to be the best at something.

If you were hired tomorrow as a football coach at a high school or college, you would want to do a good job. And there's no way around it: Doing a good job means trying to win games. But the question is: How far would you go to win? Would you push players until they wanted to scream? Would you encourage them to be dirty players? Would you tell them winning is the most important thing? Or would you let them have some fun while you were teaching them to be good football players?

The approach of a Lombardi was popular with many coaches. "Suddenly the guy coaching kids on weekends thinks he's Lombardi," Meggysey said. "He turns into a beast, yells and screams. Football is only a game, and now it ceases to be a game."

Meggysey said the joy was gone because the people in charge took the game too seriously. The cutups in locker rooms were gone, replaced by players so dedicated they forgot that it was just a game.

Football is running and jumping and grabbing people, Meggysey claimed. It's throwing and catching a ball. It shouldn't be so

serious that it doesn't have room for people who enjoy just playing as much as they enjoy winning.

Chip Oliver of the Oakland Raiders also quit, saying football had turned into a monster.

Then there was George Sauer of the New York Jets. He was one of the best pass receivers in football. He said he loved the game, but didn't like what it had become: success at any price. He said you could play your best without hating the man across from you, but that people wouldn't let you. Lombardi's "winning is the only thing" motto had taken too strong a hold, Sauer maintained.

So he quit.

31

4
The Danger

Gayle Sayers of the Chicago Bears was one of the most exciting runners of all time. His long, loping stride would take him through holes where there were no holes. A defensive back said Sayers could move sideways six feet without slowing his forward progress.

In a 1968 game in Chicago, the Bears were playing the San Francisco 49ers. Bear quarterback Virgil Carter called a basic Bear play. Sayers was to take a pitchout and carry wide behind a pulling tackle.

He took the pitch and veered to his left. His blocker was running into trouble. Sayers saw that he must cut to the inside. He planted his right foot to make the cut. But right then Kermit Alexander of the 49ers dived for him and smashed full force into Sayers' right knee.

Other players and fans remember Sayers screaming in pain. He doesn't. What he remembers is the knee wobbling when he tried to stand on it. "It's gone! It's gone!" ran through his mind. It was.

After a major operation that winter, Sayers came back for another year. But then his other knee was hit in 1970. That took two operations. He never came back again.

Gayle Sayers might have gone on to become the greatest runner ever. Instead, he retired after only five years in pro football.

"Every running back knows he's running on thin ice," Larry Csonka said. "He never knows where the big injury is waiting."

If there is one thing that all football players share, it is the knowledge that an injury might be lurking behind the next snap of the ball.

When two bodies with a total weight of about a quarter of a ton collide with a combined speed of about thirty miles an hour, something is likely to give.

Players come to expect injuries. "You can't fear them," one said, "because if you do, you can't walk out on that field." "You've got to run like you did as a kid," Jim Kiick said. And that means running without fearing anyone or anything.

"You've gotta hate that quarterback," defensive end V. Gerry Philbin of the Jets says. "I concentrate on making the quarterback fear me," says Deacon Jones of the Rams. "He has to hear footsteps," Bob Lilly of the Cowboys says of the quarterback.

Thinking like this is the start of most football injuries. These are top pro defenders talking about their job. They don't think of the quarterback as a person, he is "the quarterback." And it is their job to get him to the ground before he can pass.

In going after him, Philbin says he has to get rid of the lineman blocking him, then maybe a blocker, then he has to catch the quarterback. All this in two-and-a-half seconds. "I have to hate, otherwise I couldn't do what is necessary to do my job," adds Philbin.

And that hate means throwing the opponent to the ground. Shoving a forearm into a blocker's stomach. Lunging at a quarterback. And when 270 pounds of lineman hits

35

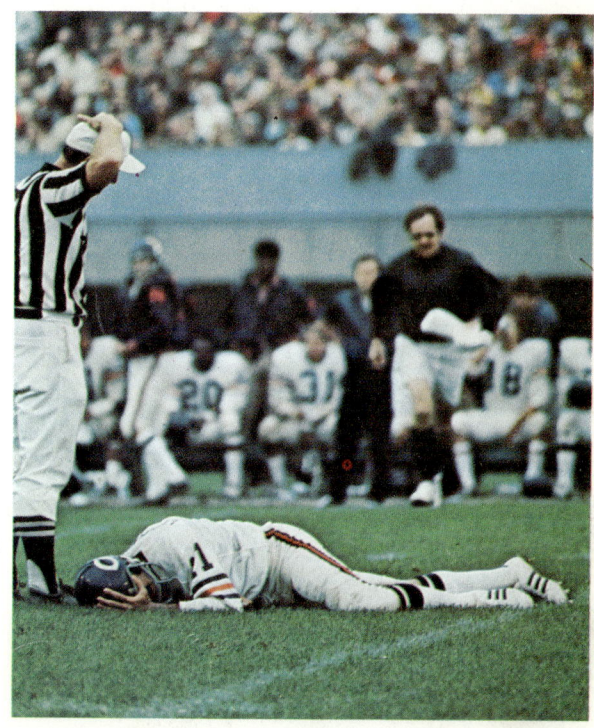

a quarterback from behind, it is no wonder that injuries occur.

"I expect to be hit," quarterback Don Meredith said. "I'm the target."

A whole football tradition has arisen about playing with injuries. Bart Starr once played an entire game with a shoulder separation. He had a bad game. After the game, Coach Lombardi raged at him: "You're playing like a cripple." Starr didn't mention the shoulder.

Players talk a lot about football injuries. And they talk about how others react to hurts. There is the story of how Sherill Headrick of Kansas City tossed off an injury.

In the middle of a tough game, Headrick suffered the worst kind of broken bone. The bone was sticking out of the ripped skin of his right thumb. On the sideline, the trainer took one look and said, "You're going to the hospital." "Quit fooling around," Headrick replied. "Grab onto it and hold it." While the trainer held the thumb, Headrick stepped back, pulling the broken bone back inside the skin. A splint was applied and the thumb was taped.

Headrick ran onto the field without missing a play.

Over the years, steps have been taken to make football safer. In the early days of football, players didn't even wear helmets. Can you imagine the Minnesota Vikings and Pittsburgh Steelers of today battering away at each other bareheaded? Rule changes have helped. The bone-crunching "flying tackle" has been outlawed. "Piling on" usually brings a fifteen-yard penalty. And there is a penalty for something called "unnecessary roughness." But these changes will never turn football into something as unrisky as chess or monopoly.

While players say they don't ever think about injuries during play, most of them believe that playing football shortens their life. "That's

37

because the body can absorb only so much punishment without giving way," one former player said. "And a year of pro ball gives a body about as much punishment as the average body gets in a lifetime."

Each year, football in America results in fifteen to twenty deaths and about fifty thousand major knee operations. John Pont of Northwestern University believes that many of them are caused by poor coaching and faulty equipment. "Some high schools and colleges just don't put enough emphasis on how to avoid injury. Many knee injuries are senseless. Kids just don't know how to protect themselves."

Sometimes pro players object to orders to play with injuries. Dick Butkus, the great middle linebacker of the Chicago Bears, sued the Bears after his career was cut short by bad legs. He claimed that his legs had been ruined by the Bears' forcing him to play while he was hurt.

Most believe that playing football cuts their life expectancy. And many are right.

The cost of play can mean more, though. It can mean hobbling through life, like Butkus, or walking on knees that have survived so many operations that you can hardly walk, like Joe Namath. Or it can mean having hands that have been so mistreated that they resemble lumps of clay, covered with bumps and callouses, like those of just about every lineman who has ever played for a long time.

And sometimes the exertion of playing football is really too much for the human body.

In a 1971 game between the Bears and Detroit Lions, a Lion receiver was hurt. A little-used substitute, twenty-eight-year-old Chuck Hughes, went into the game. The Lions were behind with time running out, but they were driving toward a touchdown. Hughes made a key catch, then he ran two deep patterns without the ball coming to him.

39

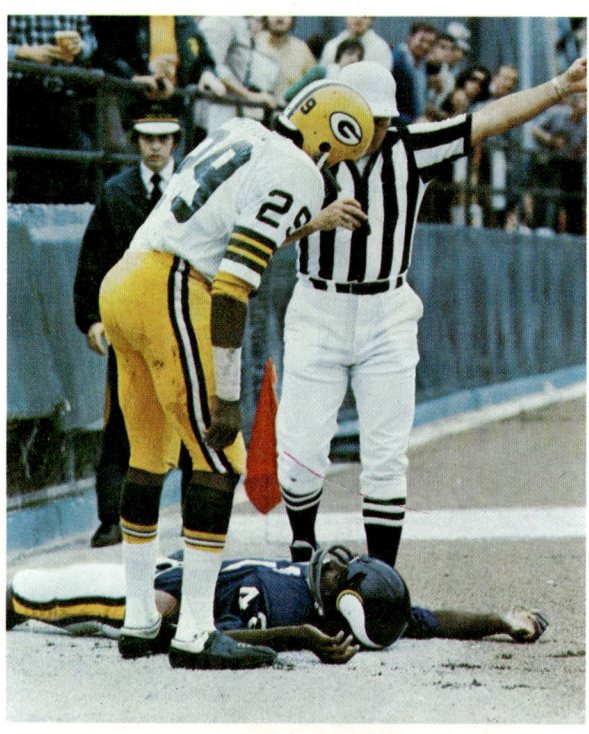

On the next play, Hughes ran a short pattern across the middle. He fell to the ground. A pass was incomplete and the play was over. Then people noticed Dick Butkus of the Bears standing over Hughes and waving his arms wildly for doctors to come out. The stands quieted as fans slowly began to realize that it was serious. The Bears' announcer Jack Brickhouse became concerned. "He hasn't moved anything since he went down," Brickhouse told the listening audience.

Chuck Hughes' heart had failed. He died.

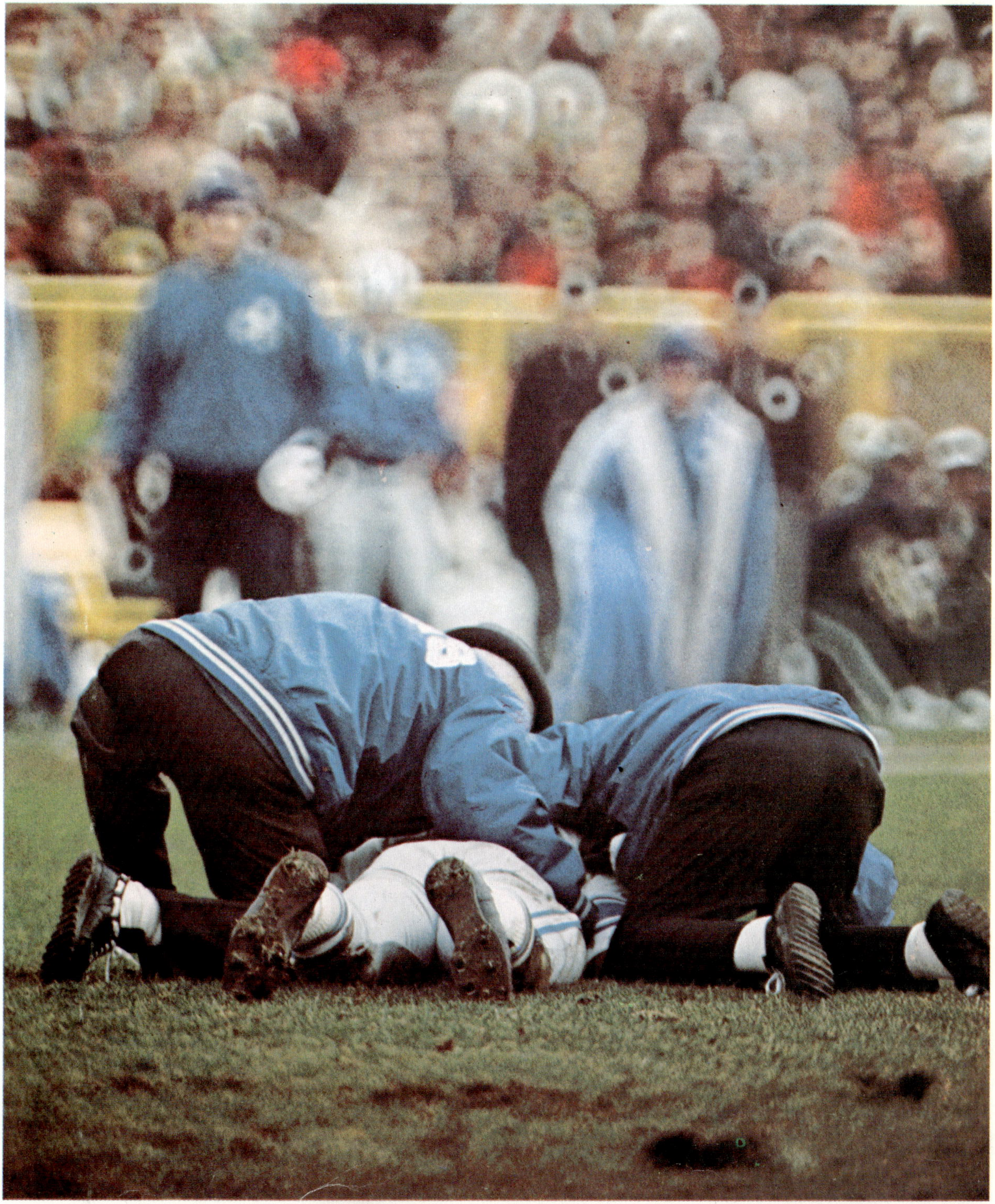

5
Why Do They Play?

Jerry Kramer of the Packers wonders about why he played football. Why did he go through the rigorous, painful training? Why did he go out on Sundays and hit and be hit by 250-pound linemen? "I don't know," he once said, "and I guess I never will."

Most players can't tell you exactly why they became football players. They may say it's because of the glory, or the money, or the love of competition. But few really know why. Football can take more from a player than it gives him. Few players get through a career without at least one major injury. Snap . . . a knee. Crunch . . . a shoulder. Some players are crippled for life.

Why do it?

Like Kramer, most never know. But some do. Quarterback Earl Morrall was talking about how times have changed. "I'm always amazed when I speak to high school youngsters and learn how carefully they have planned their lives, and how many of them look upon football or some other sport as a stepping-stone to college and a career."

Deacon Jones wouldn't be amazed. The great Los Angeles Rams lineman used football to get himself out of a life of poverty. Jones readily talks about the debt he owes football. Football was the only way he could

43

44

45

see to break away from the ghetto.

Others wouldn't be amazed either. Kramer says he used football as a way to get into college. It paid off for him. The one-time Idaho farmboy has written two books, and earned respect and financial security. He became successful in several business activities. All because of football.

"Football is a job," big defensive end Bubba Smith says. Few would disagree. The pro football player is a businessman. His business is football. It's a good business. Football players make more money than most people do. For some, the sky's the limit. Post-season games alone may bring a player more money than the average American makes in a year.

Yet many pro players don't believe that money is the most important thing in football. Mike Curtis, a very good linebacker, has said he'd play football even without any money. Curtis likes the game. He likes the contact and the challenge. Curtis became a football player because it opened up things for him. It made him a big man in high school. "I liked being a football name."

"Most players don't ever think about professional ball when they get into football," Northwestern University Athletic Director and Football Coach John Pont commented. "They simply play because they want to.

"For others," he continued, "it's to prove something to themselves or someone else." An example is Ray Nitschke. After his mother died when he was thirteen, Nitschke made sports his whole life. "It kept me going when I was down," he said. He used football to show others that he was important — "I had an inferiority complex." And the game enabled him to survive a rough childhood. He became a star in college. Later, as a pro, he was considered by many the greatest middle linebacker ever.

47

With Steve Owens, it was something else. Owens won the Heisman Trophy as the best college football player in his senior year. He set a number of NCAA rushing records at Oklahoma and won a set of cuff links given personally by the president of the United States. But when it came time for the football draft, he watched as eighteen other players (including a teammate from his Oklahoma squad) were drafted earlier. "That hurt a lot," he says now. He went into pro football with the reputation of being slow, of winning the Heisman only because of his teammates. And some people said Owens played hard only when he carried the ball.

It took him two years to shed those labels. Owens became a key man in the Detroit Lions' attack — a punishing blocker who could equally well protect a passer or wipe out defenders on a run. And his slashing, powerful running proved to be effective in the ball-control game that pro football favored. "After that draft and reading what the papers said, I had to work harder," he says. He had to prove himself to football in the only way he knew how — on the field.

"Self-confidence is one of the big things to be gained from football," Lombardi said. His prize pupil was Bart Starr. When Lombardi came to the Packers, Starr was a bench-warmer. It looked as if he would remain one until he was finally cut. After a season, Lombardi said of Starr, "This is my quarterback." And Starr became one of the all-time great ones. "I defend football, and I make no apologies for this game," Starr says. "Football gave me the confidence to know that I can do whatever I want to. I don't doubt anything."

John Pont also emphasizes that aspect of pro football. "A football player knows how to handle himself in stress situations," he said. "He is in better shape for life."

To Ray Nitschke, looking back on his twelve

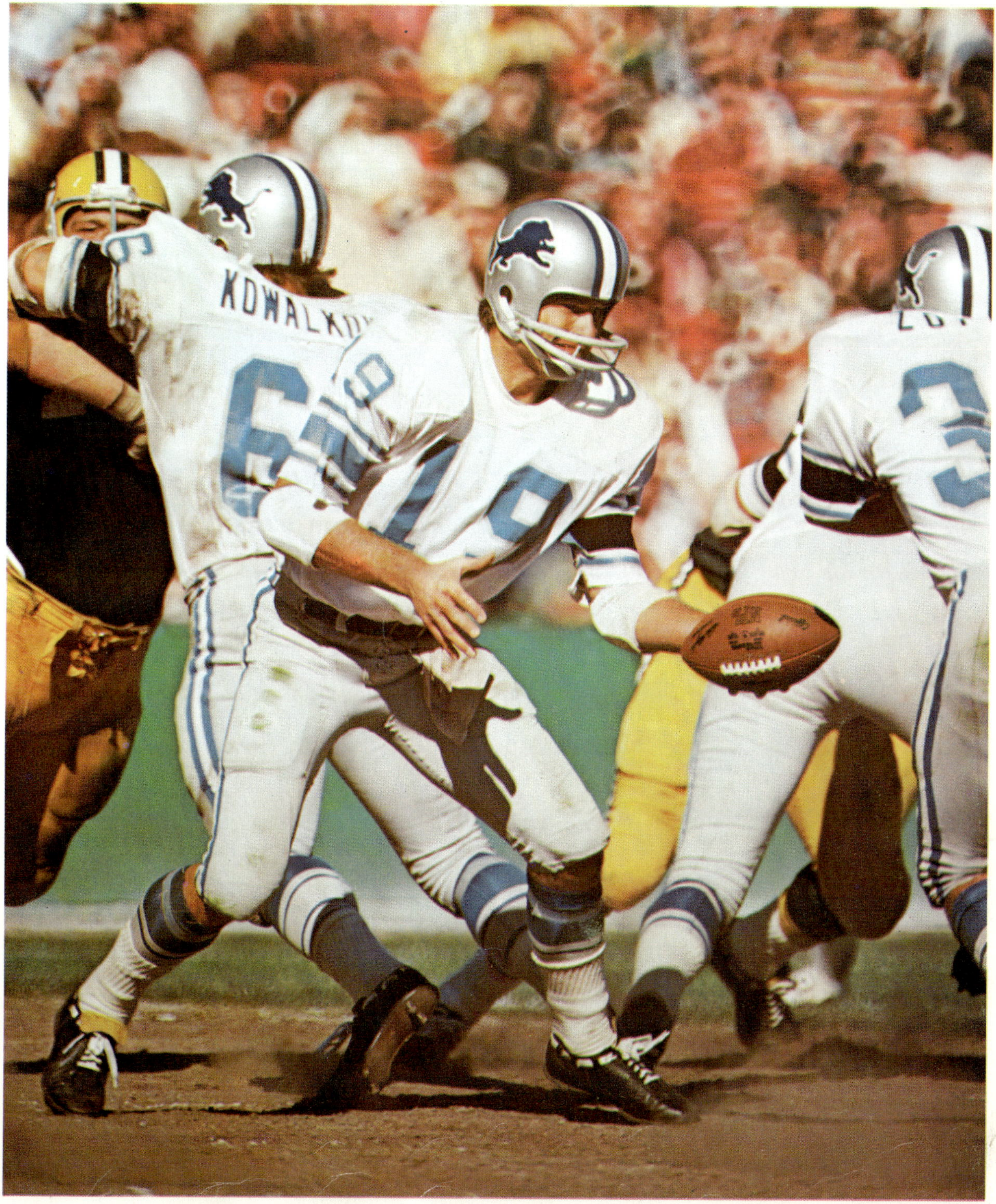

years in pro football, the reason for playing the game is easy: "I like to be the best. I like to pit myself against the best and win. When I rush a quarterback, I want him to remember Ray Nitschke even in his dreams."

That's reason enough for him.

51

6
Winners... And Losers

The Dallas Cowboys had just lost a playoff game. Quarterback Don Meredith and a couple other Cowboys walked into a restaurant and sat down to dinner. Meredith had been cheered all season as he led the Cowboys to the playoffs despite several bad injuries. Suddenly he saw another side of football. About twenty people in a corner recognized him and started to boo. They kept up their abuse until the players left. That summer Meredith retired from football.

Football is a game. In almost any game, there is a winner and a loser. The fans who hooted Meredith out of the restaurant did so because their team had lost and they blamed him for it. The criticism was unfair because football is a team game — no one player can lose a game. And Meredith had played a good game.

Bubba Smith says that a professional player's job is to win, that's what he gets paid for. But is it? Dave Meggysey argues that it is a game. That a player is paid to put out as much effort as he can to make the game interesting. If his team wins, so much the better. But there is no shame in losing, he says.

But it is a fact of life in professional football, and probably football at all levels, that life is

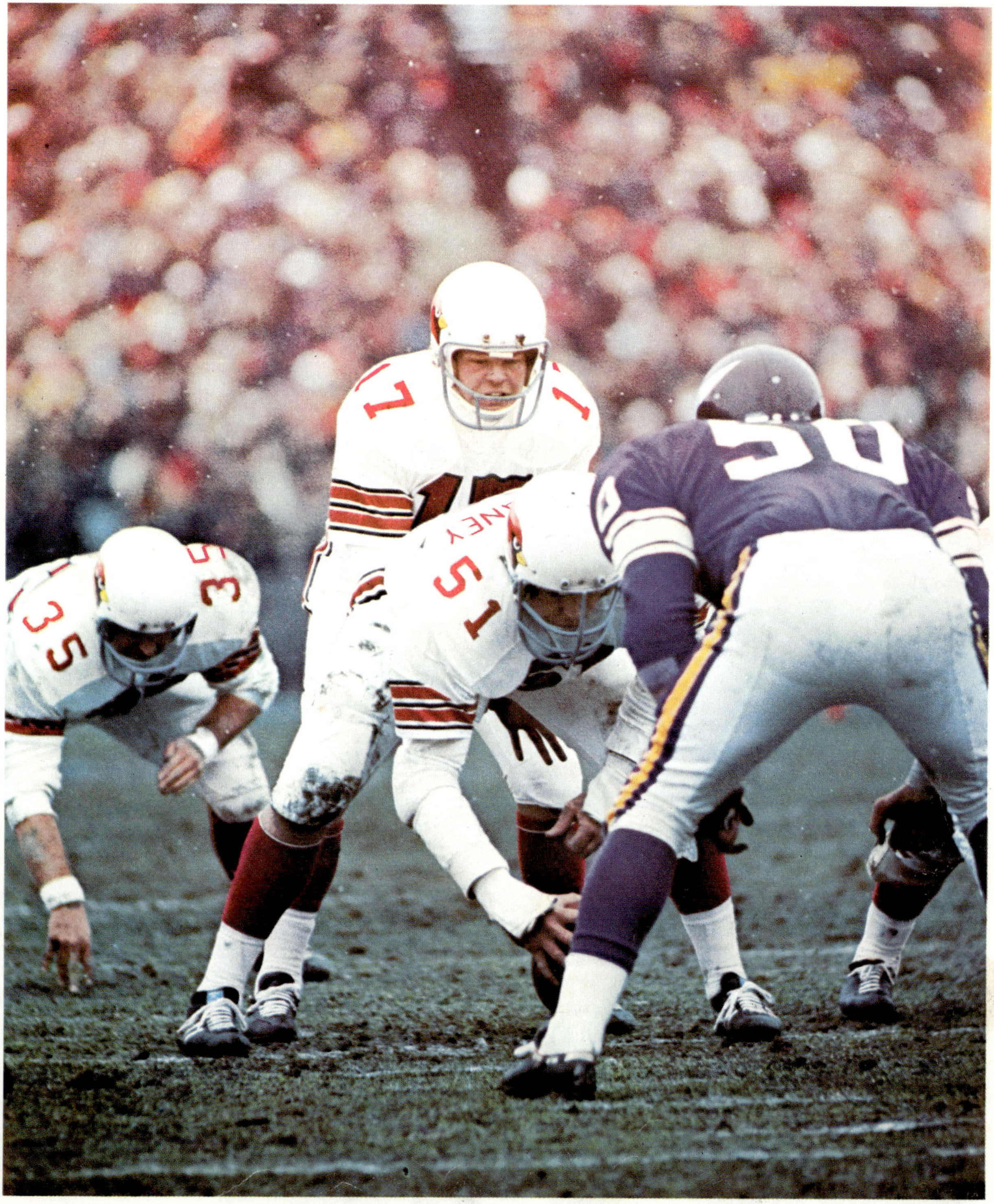
17
51
35

easier for the winners than for the losers.

In the first place, professional players are paid. And those on winning teams generally make more money than those on losing teams. In addition to the extra money they get from the playoff games, the players on the team that wins the Super Bowl split a healthy chunk of money. The losing team also gets extra money, but much less than the winners.

Earl Morrall once remarked that being with a winning team was worth twice as much as being with a losing team. Even if a player's salary wasn't high, he could make a lot from doing commercials and endorsing products.

And his career goes on. The successful player on a winning team may quickly become a top coach, or a network broadcaster, or take a high-paying job in business.

Much of this financial success comes because a winning team attracts fans. The Miami Dolphins had their first winning season, and the next year 400,000 more fans came to watch them.

This lets the team pay the players better, and it makes the player worth more when he retires. People want to listen to him broadcast a game, for instance, or they want to buy insurance from him. You never hear a broadcaster introduced as "Sam Smith, the quarterback whose team never won." No, it's the winners that are remembered.

A winning team is able to give its players more in other ways. With plenty of money to spend because fans are flocking to see the games, winning teams go first class all the way.

When Weeb Eubank was the coach of the Jets, he knew both sides of the coin. He coached the Jets when they were chronic losers and when they were on top. Things were easier when he was winning. Once, in a year when the Jets were winning, he said:

55

"I have a staff that thinks about upcoming games, one that worries about how we did in the past, and one that spends its time watching college players to see what we are going to do in the future."

It's a far cry from an earlier New York AFL team that once dressed in bushes at a park during a tryout camp. This team represents Money with a capital M. The Jets have been surrounded by one of the largest groups of nonplayers associated with any pro team. Its scouting organization is considered one of the best, and its practice facilities are among the finest.

All these things cost money — money that comes from the thousands of Jets fans. This money buys the best: top wages, top coaching, top facilities. A winning team has all three.

That's different from the losing team. Take, for example, Miami Dolphin training a few years before they became big winners. Training camps cost a lot of money — more than $75,000 for renting facilities alone. One year a group of fans offered a site at St. Petersburg, Florida, free to the Dolphins. What a deal! They jumped at the offer.

And landed on their faces.

The camp was on a beach covered by a thin layer of sod. It doesn't take much imagination to realize what would happen when 80 football players — weighing an average of 240 pounds — started running and jumping on it. The sod was soon gone, and the players began getting cut by shells in the sand. They got infections. They hurt. But, even worse, their pride was injured. For there were no dressing rooms and the players had to wash out and keep their uniforms in their motel rooms. Between the hot, humid Florida days and the wet uniforms, the motel rooms quickly became unbearable. The Dolphins moved their camp in a hurry.

That's the training camp of a loser.

57

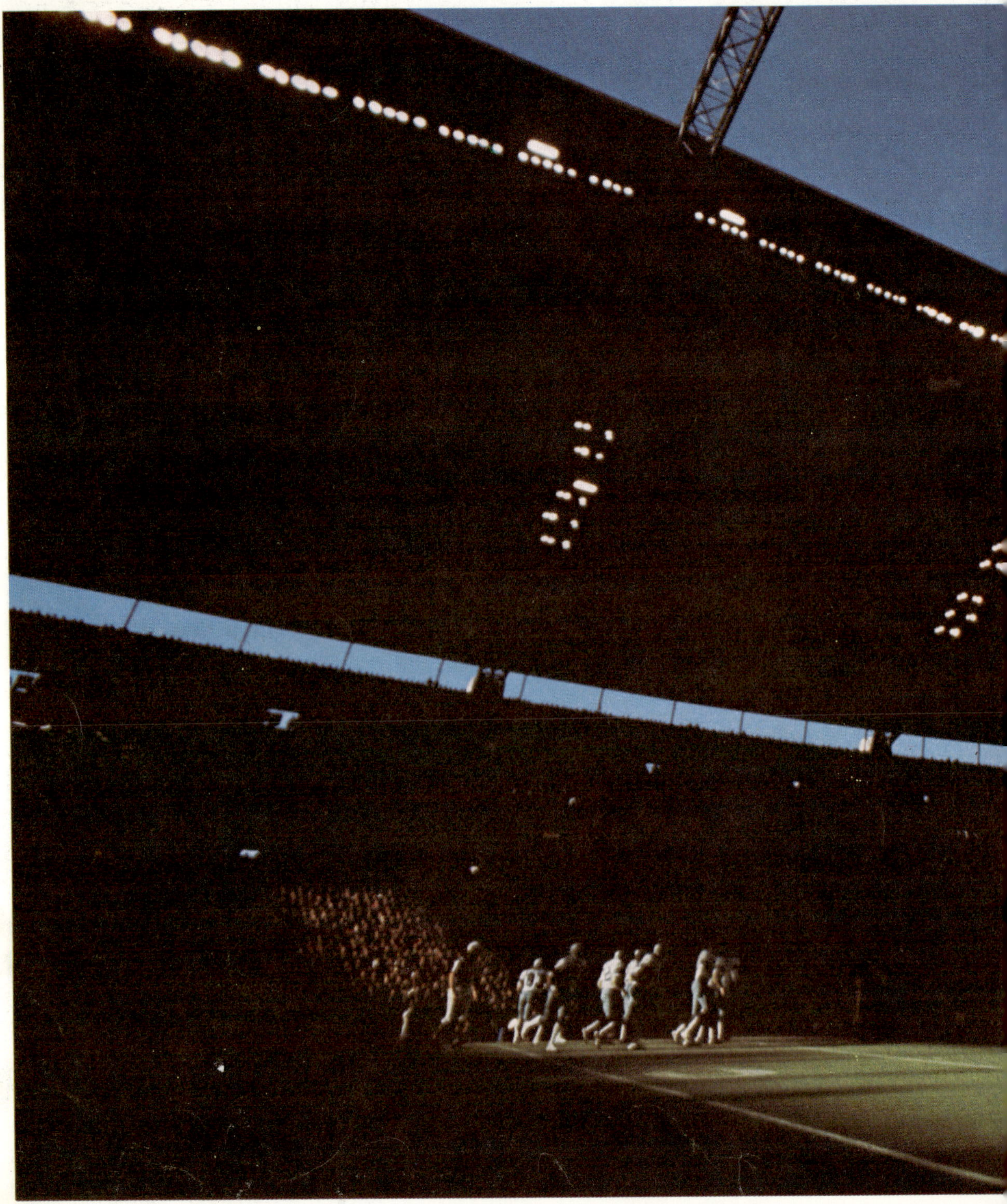

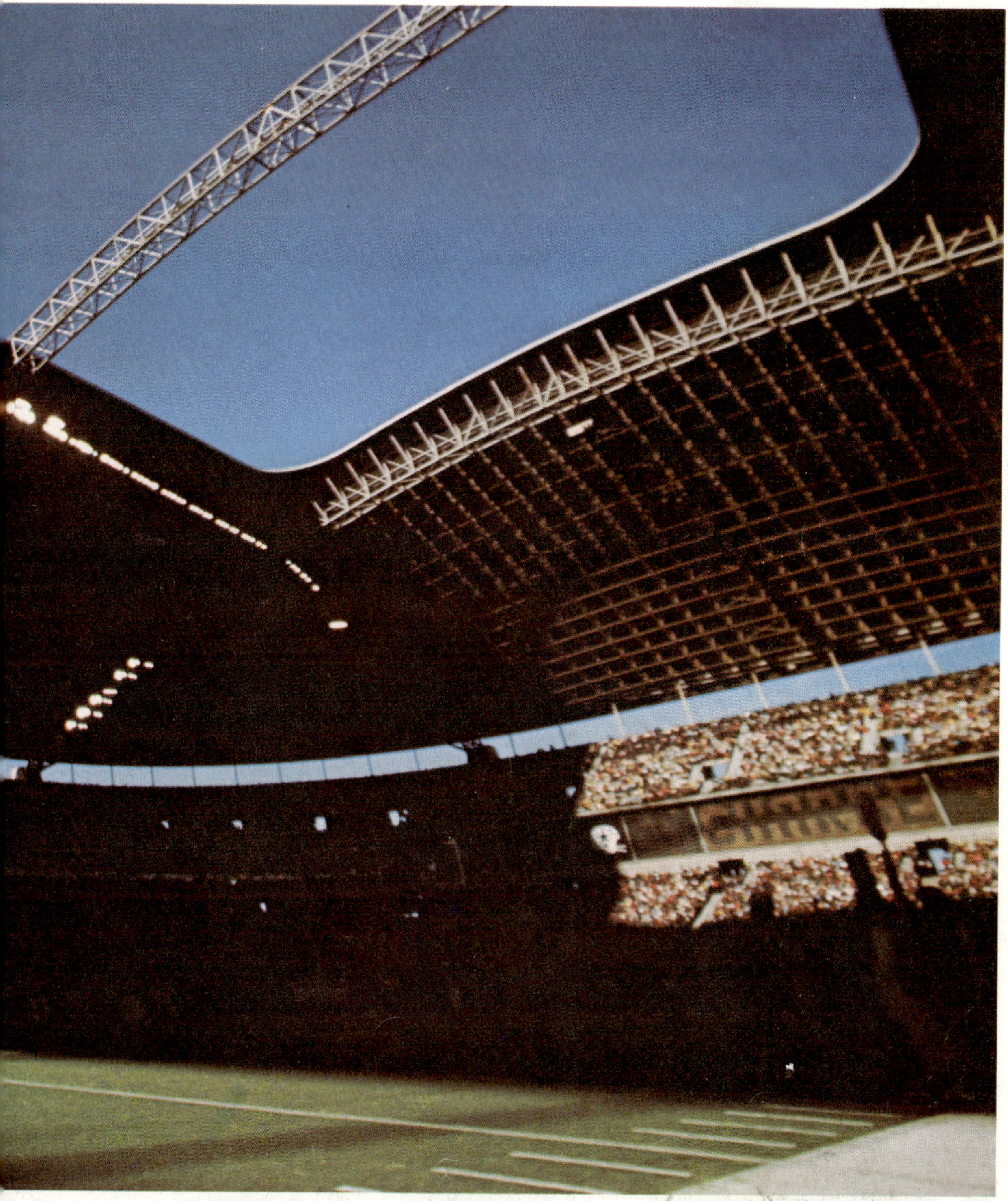

A winning team never gets its pride hurt. It is pampered by the press and the fans. Players on winning teams also have a great edge over those on losing teams: The winners have confidence.

Probably the biggest difference between winners and losers is in their attitudes. When a team loses, people look for the reason. A player's mistakes stick out a lot more when his team loses. Players on losing teams get traded. They get demoted to second string. Or, sometimes, they get released.

So losing is really toughest on the players themselves. "It's impossible to feel good after a loss," Deacon Jones says. The little hurts that a winner doesn't feel, hurt all week to a loser. It's hard to get up for games when you know your team probably won't win. In the end, it's the player who suffers most.

And sometimes it's deep suffering. Before the Packers became winners, the young daughter of one of the players came home from school one day in tears. The player asked her what was wrong. "Daddy," she asked, "are you a bum?" That hurts.

Must it be that way? What kind of a game is it where you have to be Number One or you're nothing?

Winning is part of football. It wouldn't be as good a game without it. So there will always be winners and losers.

Perhaps more credit should go to the losers. Deacon Jones didn't become a great player instantly when his team began to win. He was always a great player. But somehow the game doesn't give as much credit to great players who play for teams that lose.

There is a lot to football that is attractive. Gayle Sayers would not have tried to come back from a crippling knee injury if he hadn't loved the game. George Blanda wouldn't continue to play when he was a

61

grandfather if there wasn't a thrill to being on a football field each Sunday afternoon. Kids wouldn't play pickup games in parks and vacant lots if they didn't enjoy it.

It's fun to make a clean, crisp tackle. It's fun to crash through the line and break into an open field. It's fun to intercept a pass, to throw a perfect block, to get off a booming kick.

The Dallas Cowboys never won an NFL title while Don Meredith was with them. Once he was asked if he was disappointed about that. "Of course I wanted a title. I was sick when we lost. But it was still fun."

Despite what Lombardi said, winning isn't everything.

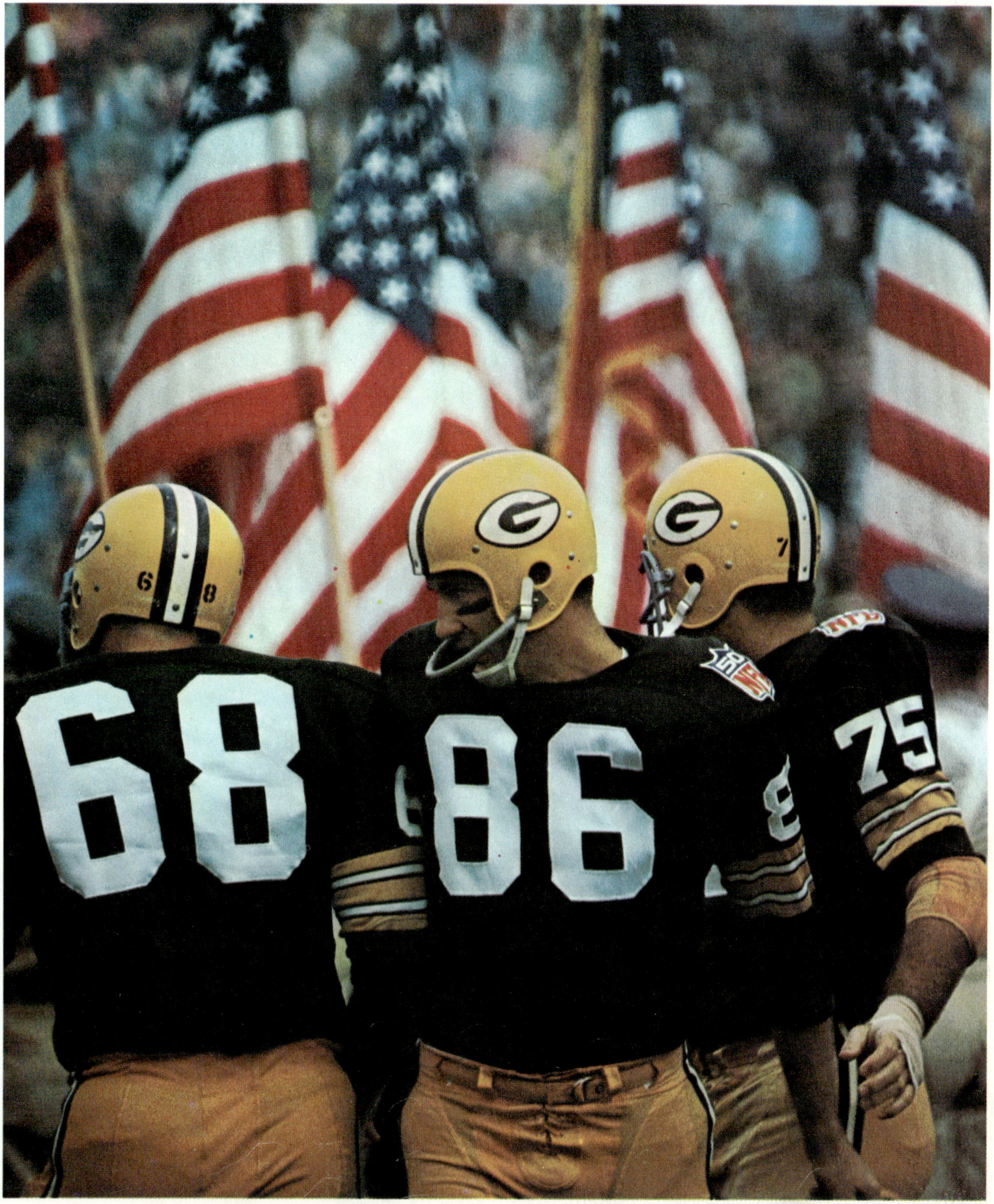
68
86
75

Pre-Reading Aids

1
A Hard Man

Purpose for Reading

Who was Vince Lombardi?
What is he most remembered for?

The answers to these questions are found in Chapter 1.

Important Vocabulary

You may find these words helpful as you read this chapter:

fearsome (fear some; fir′ səm), *adj.*
frightful, causing fear

The wounded lion was a *fearsome* sight.

desperation (des per a tion; des pə rā′ shən), *n.*
loss of hope, willingness to run any risk

In *desperation,* the kidnapped girl jumped from the speeding car.

tolerance (tol er ance; tol′ ər əns), *n.*
the ability to put up with or endure something unfavorable

His *tolerance* for pain was very high, so he did not cry out from his injuries.

perfection (per fec tion; pər fek′ shən), *n.*
highest or greatest excellence

The music teacher insisted that her two students practice and practice until they had reached the point of *perfection.*

emphasis (em pha sis; em′ fə sis), *n.*
importance, stress, special force

They placed such *emphasis* on the point that we knew it was very important to them.

Pre-Reading Aids

2
The Icebox Game

Purpose for Reading What happens when a championship game is decided on the last play?
What does it prove?

The answers are in Chapter 2.

Important Vocabulary These words may be helpful as you read:

awesome (awe some; ô′ səm), *adj.*
causing great fear, wonder, and respect

Because his knowledge of the subject was *awesome,* there were very few people who would argue with him.

conservative (con ser va tive; kən sėr′ və tiv), *adj.*
careful, cautious, free from new things

She was very *conservative* in spending her money, and so she always had some on hand.

influenced (in flu enced; in′ flü ənst), *v.*
affected, changed the behavior of

His unexpected decision *influenced* the thinking of everyone who knew him well.

factor (fac tor; fak′ tər), *n.*
something that helps to bring about a result

What she said was an important *factor* in making the decision.

triumph (tri umph; trī′ umf), *n.*
victory

Her *triumph* in the half-mile run was the result of hard work.

enforced (en forced; en fôrst′), *v.*
carried out, put into practice

The law is *enforced* by the police and the courts.

Pre-Reading Aids

3
Football Under Attack

Purpose for Reading

Is Lombardi's way of playing football the only way?
Why do some pro players quit at the height of their careers?

Read Chapter 3 to learn the answers to these questions.

Important Vocabulary

These words may be helpful as you read Chapter 3:

philosophy (phi los o phy; fə los′ə fē), *n.*
a set of beliefs that guides a person's life and actions

Martin Luther King's *philosophy* involved peaceful protest rather than violence.

humiliation (hu mil i a tion; hyü mil ē ā′shən), *n.*
a lowering of self-respect or pride

He suffered total *humiliation* when his cheating was discovered.

dedication (ded i ca tion; ded ə kā′shən), *n.*
devotion, giving oneself entirely to some purpose

He learned too late that his *dedication* to making money had left him too little time for anything else.

discipline (dis ci pline; dis′ə plin), *n.*
training of the mind, a trained condition involving order and obedience

The sergeant considered strict *discipline* to be the most important part of military training.

dehumanizing (de hu man iz ing; de hyü′mə nīz ing), *adj.*
brutal, lacking human qualities

Her trip to the ancient prison convinced her that being a prisoner there must have been a *dehumanizing* experience.

violence (vi o lence; vī′ə ləns), *n.*
rough force

Joan was opposed to *violence* because she thought that her goals could be reached peacefully.

cutups (cut ups; kut′ups), *n.*
people who show off or play tricks

The *cutups* on the team could be annoying, but now that they were gone no one seemed to laugh much any more.

Pre-Reading Aids

4
The Danger

Purpose for Reading

How dangerous is football?

You'll find the answer in Chapter 4.

Important Vocabulary

You may find the following words of help as you read this chapter:

injury (in ju ry; in′jər ē), *n.*
damage, harm, hurt

Mr. Walters escaped serious *injury* when his car struck a tree.

lurking (lurk ing; lėrk′ing), *v.*
waiting out of sight

There was great danger *lurking* about her if she made a mistake.

tradition (tra di tion; trə dish′ən), *n.*
a way of thinking, a belief or custom handed down from one generation to the next

It was a *tradition* in their family to get together for the holidays each year.

absorb (ab sorb; ab sôrb′), *v.*
to take in or endure

The fighter could *absorb* a great deal of punishment without slowing down.

exertion (ex er tion; eg zėr′shən), *n.*
effort, strenuous action

The *exertion* of winning the race drained her of all her energy.

Pre-Reading Aids

5
Who Do They Play?

Purpose for Reading

Why do grown men play professional football?

The answer to this question can be found in Chapter 5.

Important Vocabulary

The following words may be of help to you as you read:

poverty (pov er ty; pov′ər tē), *n.*
the condition of being poor

Their extreme *poverty* made it impossible to buy enough clothing and food.

ghetto (ghet to; get′ō), *n.*
a part of a city where a minority group live because of economic, social, or legal pressures

The *ghetto* begins just outside the main business area of the city.

financial (fi nan cial; fə nan′shəl), *adj.*
having to do with money

Joe lacked sense about *financial* matters, and so he spent all of his savings foolishly.

security (se cu ri ty; si kyúr′ə tē), *n.*
freedom from care or fear

Judy had a feeling of *security* because of the money she had so carefully saved.

inferiority complex (in fe ri or i ty com plex; in fir ē ôr′ə tē kom′pleks), *n.*
a feeling of being less good or less important than other people

He had developed an *inferiority complex* from his many failures in school.

self-confidence (self con fi dence; self kon′fə dəns), *n.*
belief in one's own ability

She was successful in so many things that she had developed a feeling of great *self-confidence* about her ability to succeed in new areas.

Pre-Reading Aids

6
Winners... And Losers

Purpose for Reading

How important is winning to a professional football player and team?

You'll find the answer to this question as you read Chapter 6.

Important Vocabulary

The following words may prove helpful as you read this chapter:

despite (de spite; di spīt′), *prep.*
in spite of, regardless of

He stayed overnight *despite* the fact that he knew his parents did not want him to.

abuse (a buse; ə byüs′), *n.*
harsh treatment

He didn't say anything, but his *abuse* of the dog made it clear that he was angry.

commercials (com mer cials; kə mer′shəlz), *n.*
advertisements on radio or TV

Television *commercials* often have a strong effect on what products we buy.

retires (re tires; ri tīrz′), *v.*
gives up his job

When she *retires,* she hopes to spend her time traveling and reading.

pampered (pam pered; pam′pərd), *v.*
spoiled, treated too nicely

She had been so *pampered* by her parents that she was not able to take care of herself when it was necessary.

credit (cred it; kred′it), *n.*
praise, recognition

John was given *credit* by everyone for the success of the soccer team.

71

Discussion Questions

Chapter 1
Who among your friends is most like Vince Lombardi? In what ways?

Chapter 2
If you were asked to react to the statement that the Green Bay-Dallas championship game didn't prove a thing, what would you say?

Chapter 3
What might have happened if Lombardi and Meggysey had met? What might have been said?

Chapter 4
How would you persuade a community worried about football injuries that a team should be started in their school?

Chapter 5
Do you think that the rewards of football are worth the risk of injury? Are there jobs without the risk of injury that offer the same rewards?

Chapter 6
Is it fair that the professional football team with the poorest record has the first choice to draft college football players each year? If you were chosen by a losing team, what would you lose or gain?

Related Activities

If you enjoy football, or want to learn more about it, you may want to do one or more of the following:

1. Make a glossary of football terms that would be helpful to someone who is unfamiliar with the game.

2. Develop a chart showing the hand signals used by football officials. Explain these signals to your class.

3. Go to your school or public library. Make a list of the magazine articles and books about Vince Lombardi. If only a few sources are available, work with the librarian to determine what materials might be added to the collection.

4. Create a Football-Bingo game, using football terms and their definitions, rather than numbers and letters.

5. Write to the Pro Football Hall of Fame in Canton, Ohio. Ask for information about one or more of the following:
   the date of founding and the purpose of the Pro Football Hall of Fame
   procedures for electing members
   contents of the museum
   other matters of interest
   Report your findings to your class.

6. On a map of the United States, locate the home cities of the NFL football teams. Label each location with the team name, the name of the stadium, and the stadium's seating capacity. Ask your librarian for help in locating this information.

7. Invite a football coach, game official, or player to speak to your class or school. Suggest a topic which interests you and your classmates. Introduce your guest and be sure to write a follow-up letter of thanks.

8. Interview a football coach, official, or player. Record the interview for presentation to your class. Or, write up the interview, perhaps for publication in your school or local newspaper.

9. Go to a game and prepare a tape recording of the sounds of football. Play this for your class. Explain what the sounds are.

10. Visit your school or local library and try to find how and where football began. Ask your librarian for assistance. Be sure to use more than one source. Summarize your findings and present them to your class, in oral or written form.

11. Conduct a poll of football coaches and players. Why do they think playing football is worthwhile? How important is winning to them? Make the results of your poll available to your class. Or, write up your results for use by your school or local newspaper.

12. Obtain a copy of the *Official National Football League Guide* from the New American Library. (Ask your librarian for assistance in locating the address.) Look through your copy. Then tell your classmates what it contains and make it available for their use.

13. Make and post a list of Super Bowl statistics for the past several years. Include the names of teams, locations of games, scores, and other information that interests you.

14. Collect pictures that capture the feeling of football from sports magazines and other sources. Try to focus on a single theme (for example, the brutality of football, the excitement of football, or the desire to win). Display your pictures in your classroom.

15. Make and post a list of professional football records. You may want to include such things as:
most yards gained rushing in a single game
most yards gained rushing in a single season
most yards gained rushing in a career
best passing percentage in a single game
best passing percentage in a single season

16. Watch the newspapers and sports magazines for articles about football. Clip and post them in your class regularly. You may want to report now and then about what is happening.

17. Diagram two or more football plays. Explain these to members of your class. As a result of your explanations, the class should be able to read similar diagrams.

18. Write to NFL headquarters. (Your librarian can help you find the address.) Inquire about some or all of the following:
official rules
statistics regarding players' salaries
statistics regarding players' injuries
responsibilities of the Commissioner
other matters of interest to you
Make your findings available to your classmates.

19. Interview the team doctor of a football team. Ask about the number and kind of injuries treated in recent years. Get the doctor's opinion about the dangers of football. Make the results of your interview available to your class or school.

20. Draw several cartoons about football. If you prefer, draw a comic strip or two.

Reading and Curriculum Editor	Peter Sanders, PhD. Wayne State University
Associate Reading Consultants	John Clark, M.A. Cincinnati Public Schools Cincinnati, Ohio Edward Daughtrey, M.S. Norfolk City Schools Norfolk, Virginia
Story Editor	Patrick Reardon
Associate Editor	Deborah Gardner
Coordinator of Learner Verification	Peter Sanders, PhD.
Related Activities and Vocabulary Sections	Peter Sanders, PhD.
Photography Editor	Eric Bartelt
Graphic Design	Interface Design Group, Inc.

Color Process	American Color Systems
Lithography	A. Hoen & Co.
Binding	Lake Book Bindery

Manufactured in the United States of America to Class A specifications of The Book Manufacturers' Institute

2 3 4 5 6 7 8 9 0   80 79 78 77 76